7.95

58u

DATE DUE

DEMCO

SAINTS IN THEIR OX-HIDE BOAT

A POEM BY

BRENDAN GALVIN

LOUISIANA STATE UNIVERSITY PRESS   Baton Rouge and London
1992

Manufactured in the United States of America
First printing
01 00 99 98 97 96 95 94 93 92   5 4 3 2 1

Designer: Amanda McDonald Key
Typeface: Palatino
Typesetter: Graphic Composition, Inc.
Printer and binder: Thomson-Shore, Inc.

Library of Congress Cataloging-in-Publication Data
Galvin, Brendan.
    Saints in their ox-hide boat : a poem / by Brendan Galvin.
      p.   cm.
    ISBN 0-8071-1694-7.—ISBN 0-8071-1695-5 (pbk.)
    1. Brendan, Saint, the Voyager, ca. 483–577—Poetry. 2. America—
Discovery and exploration—Irish—Poetry. I. Title.
    PS3557.A44S25 1992
    811'.54—dc20   91-35822
                                           CIP

Selections from this poem appeared originally in *Caesura, Poet and Critic, Southern Humanities Review,* and *Tar River Poetry,* and in *Outer Life: The Poetry of Brendan Galvin* (Ampersand Press, 1991). The author is grateful to the editors for permission to reprint those selections here.

The author also offers thanks to the John Simon Guggenheim Memorial Foundation and the National Endowment for the Arts for fellowships that enabled him to complete this poem, and to Central Connecticut State University for research support.

The paper in this book meets the guidelines for permanence and durability of the Committee on Production Guidelines for Book Longevity of the Council on Library Resources. ⊗

For Bill, Diane, and Molly
Blue water folk themselves

FROM IRISH MONASTICISM CAME THE IDEA OF "white martyrdom," of giving up all that one loves by leaving one's religious brethren, kin, and homeland for a solitude in a foreign country or on an island, the better to contemplate God without distractions. If such a pilgrimage was by sea, it was sometimes called a "blue martyrdom," and the most famous of the blue martyrs was the man known now as St. Brendan the Navigator. Born around 484 near Tralee, County Kerry, Brendan established monastic foundations in Scotland, Wales, Brittany, and quite probably the Faroe Islands, as well as Ireland, and his influence spread about the European continent and as far north as the Gulf of Finland. Up to the sixteenth century, he occupied the place in Irish hagiography now reserved for St. Patrick.

We know of Brendan's exploits primarily through the Latin *Voyage of St. Brendan*, written in Ireland perhaps as early as 800, and from various *Lives* and versions of his adventures popular all over Europe throughout the Middle Ages. A reference to his confrontation with a whale appears on the 1513 map of an Ottoman sea captain, and some maps of the Atlantic speculated on the location of a "St. Brendan's Isle" well into the eighteenth century.

How far, in reality, did Brendan sail? We know that Irish monks had lived in the islands off Iceland's coast prior to the Norse arrival there, hence the Vestmannaeyjar (West Men's or Irishmen's) Islands, with their remnant bells and croziers in the Irish manner. Much has been made of the idea that the Promised Land that Brendan's sea-drift monks visited in the *Voyage* was actually somewhere in the New World. In 1976–1977, Tim Severin and his crew, in a vessel approximating those used by the monks—a large ocean-going curragh of tanned ox hides covering a frame of oak and ash, the hull soaked in and regularly replenished with sheep grease for waterproofing—sailed from Ireland along a stepping-stone route, going north to the Hebrides, Faroes, and Iceland, then south under Greenland to the coast of Newfoundland. Severin's feat and subsequent book, *The Brendan Voyage* (1978), not only proved such a journey possible but verified logically some of what appears to be a fictitious, sometimes miraculous sequence of events and encounters in the original Latin *Voyage of St. Brendan*.

While *Saints in Their Ox-Hide Boat* draws on some of the broad details of both the Severin adventure and the anonymous Latin *Voyage*, the characters of Brendan and his monks are my inventions, as are most of the incidents in the poem. One must keep constantly in mind that these men were both religious contemplatives and hardy sailors in a time when no clear distinction between early Christian and late pagan can be drawn, and when monks were sometimes called upon to war for their secular lords.

Likewise, we should not think of them as conforming to a central religious authority. From the time of Christianity's arrival on Irish soil until well after the Synod of Whitby (664) attempted to enforce Roman observances, the faith there was largely supported and spread by monastic houses that sprang up throughout the country. Each was autonomous under the rule of a charismatic abbot, and evolved a liturgy of its own. The combination of spiritual rule and human exemplar was attractive to the Irish, and the monastic foundations were magnets for numerous recruits. Despite an abbot's wish to maintain a small community, his own holiness often drew many to him. We know very little about the foundations' rituals and prayers; that they were not those prescribed by Rome may be evidenced by the fact that even English Jesuits, entering Ireland after Queen Elizabeth's reign, could not recognize some of the ceremonies of Gaelic-speaking believers. To some degree,

Rome and her Irish bishops were looked upon as meddlesome, and in Ireland ecclesiastical power was usually held by the local abbot rather than the resident bishop.

B.G.

SAINTS IN THEIR OX-HIDE BOAT

[Clonfert Abbey, A.D. 578]

Without fail these three things
will assure an unlucky sailing:
turning the boat sunward through
three right-hand circles
and standing out of harbor
before the Beltane fires are dead
on spring hillsides; turning your face
toward the waves without prayers
and a fast, for that sea is
no Christian, or brother to any man,
but at best's an uneasy accomplice
who lays no gift of salmon on
anyone's threshold; and taking aboard
a crewman with an edge to his tongue
like a cat's. A boat wants
men who are nimble of mind
and hop spry to orders, no debtors,
fumblers, braggarts, bishops, or loons
to tempt the waters, but a few
with sense, long on muscle and oak,
and better a sharp novice than
two experienced bleaters
whose work is all in their mouths.

My boy, I lay these doings out for you
because I know you were raised
among fields and hills and never
beat your way north beyond the Sheep Islands
or south around Ireland to Wales and Brittany,
and ask that you copy all I tell you

without amendment, whether you consider it
fantastical, or not fantastical enough,
a white head's inventions, who, though
yet sound in body, gapes in his mind
and toothless mouth.

First day of the week, and best
for a journey, before any lark
shook awake to welcome the light,
I followed the stream's waver and spill
among harebells and green thrift,
those little red huts of the blossoming
fuchsia, and avens and sorrel,
down the mountain. All the way
through wet heather, I warmed
into the walk, working my neck
and shoulders to unknot them from a night
on my stone pillow, swinging
my leather satchel past sheep-stare
and sheep-stare, the identical
dumb questions from black faces,
and dropped down out of a cowl of
mist to where the sea was working away
at its niche in the rock, still
and forever honing its discontent,
for all its time in the world.
Our boat waited, ready with water
and mass wine in goatskins, sacked
onions and flat oat loaves, hazelnuts,
dried fish, parsnips, lave, dulse,
and blue sea holly against
the swollen-gum sickness, and a flask
of holy water tucked beneath
the ox skull on her prow.

Singing through the mist came Owen,
a white lucky stone on his neck thong.
No matter how long and well they have
paid with the small of their backs
at an oar, God-burnt and sunburnt,
these old monks are brief sleepers,
and Owen I picked over quicker men
for his wind- and water-reading eye.
It was he that taught me to determine
north by grabbing a louse off myself
and watching how its head
always returns to that direction.
Now Martin—the warrior who came
gore-sick to our abbey and asked
to be taken in, and who no man discovered
in drink from that day—new fish spears
in hand, and limber to risk an arm
at stepping the mast or changing sail.

— Last night, Abbot, he said,
I dreamed a flock of sheep on Eagle Mountain,
wide as a lap of snow across its slope.

A good sign, I nodded, easeless as always
before faring out, and because
I knew what was coming next.

— Ah, but were they climbing the mountain
or coming down? asked Owen.

— What matter is that? I said.

— Well, you see, Brendan, if those sheep
were moving toward higher pasture,
it would mean well for our journey.
But if Martin dreamed them driving

down the hillside, as though
the herdsman's dog was in it . . .

I raised my hand, and would hear no more,
for next he'd be interpreting our sneezes.
Now the shipwright Diarmuid and young
Conor approached with their gear
in satchels, and Conor an otter's pelt
about his waist, for luck. Two
outward-looking men, high-hearted,
each with his ray of sense, sturdy of
mind to endure those times at sea
when all the voices of the past
come out of memory and lurk, laughing
or crying, telling whatever it is
they tell from a blue-black squall
bruising the sky above the mast.
Frisky as goats these two were,
like all young men without women,
like yourself perhaps, though I've
seen no evidence of it. But you too
may be ready on the day when
you have to stand in the gap. Last was
bald Cernan, the smith, a silent man
and intent, as though to tip the cauldron
of his thoughts might spill it all.
Maker of fishhooks, tooth-giver to saws,
tooth-taker from the screeching mouths
of monks, bonesetter, canny with fish oils
at easing strained limbs and quelling
headaches. For all his power above
iron and fire, one faint lift of the head
was his greeting all around.

— Father, Diarmuid said, as I came out
the clochan door a cock crowed.

My head began its swimming. Then Conor,
stitcher of boatskins:

— When I rose from my oatcakes, my stool
heeled over as though some unseen hand
were in the situation.

As always, the old persuasion here,
and best stepped lightly around, if ever
we were to get on the water.

— No good will come of our dipping a single oar
this day, announced Owen. A nod went round
the knot of men, and since that looked to be
the drift of it, we would try again tomorrow,
for whoever would go looking for sanctum
over seas had best begin on a firm right foot.

And why turn my back on Ireland again
to tempt that ocean with the souls of these
five monks? To cancel with music
a curragh makes on the waves
the hammering and dust of our community,
overrun by recruits slack-jawed with admiration
and always in the way—so many you'd think
nobody ever died—and the endless talk
that runs around in circles like those
pocked in stone by the first people?
Or to break from that abbey's yoke
out across limits to where sand, sea,
rock, and sky scrub acedia from the mind,
and point a new way to God, who is a fire

that shapes Himself different on whatever
path He's approached by, yet stays the same?
Or to tangle my spirit in nets of pride?
Nights on the mountain, I churned these questions
without arriving at a solid answer.

Next morning Martin waited by the curragh,
up to his knees in the creek, imploring
help for our journey, his arms spread like
our Master's on His Cross. Conor and Owen
clattered over the stones, and soon
all six were gathered.

— Into the boat, I ordered.

— Good fortune, Diarmuid replied, as if to
make restitution for yesterday. Already
I have seen a raven hopping about
my path, white feathers in his wings.

— But a little bright-headed wren
called to me on the way, Conor said.

— Now here is a case where the one may
cancel the other, Owen began. But from
what direction did the little one call?
For if it called from the north, then
a visit from in-laws may be expected.

— He has no in-laws, he's a celibate monk!
I shouted. Ah, the little bird-faced man.
I thought to give him a thump
to shut him up.

— Then it were best we sail toward the south,
Owen replied.

— We are sailing north, I said, fearing
my red beard and tonsure of those days
would crackle and burn off like straw on fire,
leaving me bare skulled as Cernan, who now,
discomfited, was staring from us at the creek.

— But if that wren called from the west,
Owen went on, then perhaps we should not
sail at all, since there are only fields
and mountains to the east. And death tidings
are on us if it called from the ground
or a cross, and the drowning of many
if it called from the resting places of
our brethren by the abbey. Of course
it is of no consequence to us at all
if it called from the south, for that means
a sickness or wolves among the herds,
and we would be on the sea . . .

Old man, in truth we are both too far gone
for a sail toward the sun's resting place,
which may only be a fool's long errand
toward the grave or beyond, and it's better
we both were tending lambs and onions
over there behind the cashel wall.

Those were my thoughts, but here's
what I said: — Tonight we'll go
sleepless and full of prayers together
on the mountain, that no one dream
a drove of pigs or a girl in a red petticoat.
Keep watch. Should one or another begin
blinking off, give him your sharpest elbow
with my blessing. We'll fast, so none upsets

the salt, and pray against seeing
the lame woman Maire Dubh cross a deathlook
with us before we enter the curragh
tomorrow morning. An unlikely event anyhow,
in fog and that far up the mountain.

All the path down to sunlight I prayed through
a mist so woolly no bird, sheep, shepherd,
birdcall, rare-colored stone, or calf
was seen or heard, not even a bee
humming about the pleasures of its labor.
There were tide glints as from
an archangel's breastplate when we made the boat.

— Now, to your places! Wading in, I took the tiller.

Four trimmed their oars, and Conor cast us
off, but before I could stop him
leapt in over the curragh's left side.

— The devil from us if that doesn't call
a halt to it, Owen cried. At the oars
they all four sat openmouthed
and round-eyed as those stone heads
that sit staring about our hills.

— Bruising and breaking of bones on
whoever lifts a leg over that rail!
I bellowed into their faces. We are
going down this creek!

And so whatever way clouds went, we went.
Call it cracking a knee to God's power
if you like, since nowhere
is it more manifest than on that ocean,
but what were our choices when
no curragh can sail head to the wind
anyway? Islands waited, one
under every cloud that stood
building on itself as though moored,
while all the other clouds rushed on.
When gannet Christ, walking a wave
of air, claps wings and spears through
your ribs for your soul, you are less
than a clutch of fish bones
washed up on the world, with no
earthly purpose save to deny the lit
eye of a woman and the poured-milk
turn of her neck. Neither hills like
paps of Danu nor fields potent with mares
nor tables buckling under spread
feasts provoke you, but grip, hilt,
and blade, the cross is a sword
turned against this life, and you dream
in your stone beehive of islands:
shag-defended heights backlit by evening;
rocky stacks; mere humps supporting
washed-up mats of scraw; landfalls of
sheep fat as cattle; egg islands
where, flapping your arms, you drive birds off
and fill your baskets for the change
of diet; treeless anvil shapes without
anchorage; tern-swarmed beaches; skerries;
a narrow stretch between rockfaces
riddled with caves, fast water reeled over
by a dinning stir of gulls, gannets,
puffins, guillemots, skuas—and then
that island you never dream, the one

you'll know only when you wade ashore
and feel, among the bindweed and reddening
ferns, in the silence of lichen-flowering
stones, like a trespasser on some
lump of everlastingness. You'll never know
unless you drop that quill and sail, my boy.

We met no monks offering bread, no otters
that led us to clear wells, but scavenged
winkles on what strands we could,
dropped bait and fished, trolled fish
when a fulmar trailed our wake. One day
far on in summer, in fog so thick you couldn't
find your eye with your thumb, we heard
voices in antiphon traveling across water,
monks singing, but as we closed on them
more as if folk had convened on a festival day,
each agreed to sing his favorite air
at the same time. Nearer, it turned pandemony:

— The punished dead, howling and slobbering around
with Pilate and Judas, enisled here for eternity,
Owen cried, churning his ancient hands.

That old man could talk the sea up a duck's arse,
God rest him, even fed the others once
when we ran up on an island bejumping
with rabbits that the poor creatures
were witches. He was handy to whistle up
a breeze when we were becalmed
as swans in a lough, but sometimes his
delusions found soft nests in his brothers'
minds. The singing that chilled us so
came from a rock pile where the seals

hauled out to try their human voices.
Owen sang back, of course, as we passed,
nothing I could sing you now,
but a kind of babbling a child
in his bath in the stream might make,
sounds you might like to hear, but nothing
in any tongue I know about,
until their music faded off our stern.

Don't mis-hear an old man and set it down
that we came across souls out there.
They were as surely seals as those
radiant blobs we sometimes plowed
our way through in the dark were jellyfish,
not souls. Seals, I said, not souls.
But you may have heard—nor would I
be putting an egg in your cowl,
for I tell you truly—that on the north leg
of our voyage sometimes an island floated
on the sky. You could see a band of light
between it and the water, and if it was
a cloud it was one with brown hills on it,
and grass above the shoreline. This
we pursued for days without reward,
since we never seemed to gain on it,
perhaps because it traveled faster than
the curragh. Though when I thought about it
afterwards, how would we get up on it
if ever we caught it? Such sights would knock
you dead, it seems like, until you see
the next thing. One morning when Cernan
was on watch, he shook me from sleep.

    You'll never believe this one, Brendan.

There on the sky, another island! Floating
upside down, its peak dangling like
a blue turnip over the waves! By your face
I can see you believe I'm doing the leg pull
on a poor boy too long in the scriptorium.
Not so. You know how its body joins
the two wings of a butterfly? Imagine
two islands then, attached at their bases,
or one doubling itself, up in the air!

In those far waters things better than
miracles appear, as though to prove
the world can supply whatever
a wandering mind might devise. One day
a brother cried from the bow
that a curragh was approaching.
Who else could have crossed that far, daring
the North beyond flaming mountains, and now
returning in trouble? She rolled too severely
for conditions, at times laid over
on one cheek, the bow lifting sometimes
as though a following sea had boarded,
swamping and righting herself as she came.

— Prepare to take her people off, I shouted,
and the crew moved to the rail. She passed us
to starboard, a chunk of hull-shaped
groaning ice, that's all. Astonishments
everywhere. Here will be the head of
a swimming horse, there a man on a rock,
gesturing like some poet spouting off
at court for an extra cupful, even as
he wobbles and sinks in a field
of minor lumps like rafts of fowl at rest.

Had I in the flesh the ice cattle I've seen
through mist, I'd be king of all Munster;
Bishop of Rome if I ruled over half
the ice clochans and oratories we outsteered
while our hull plowed the slush mumbling
and crackling against it, at times sounding
like an invisible host whose boundaries
we had violated, muttering one long
threat against the boatskin
as we steered among the statues,
poling them off our bows. White
in the distance, towered and fortified,
a dwelling place shone, seeming to draw
all sunlight to itself. This could be
that island, was my thought.

— What king's rath might that be, Diarmuid wondered
aloud, of such bright stone?

Owen I kept my eye on, ready to clap
his gob shut, as well he knew
by the look of him.

— Let us hope those who live there are Christian men,
said Martin, who had abjured all battles forever.

Its nearness proved another trick of that sea,
since all the day and into the next
we chased it without seeming to advance,
as when for the first time you sight the Rock
of Patrick and set out for it, only to learn
that the plains of Tipperary weren't made
to pleasure your feet. Nearer, we dropped sail
and drifted in such brilliance as

we had never seen. That whiteness drew
all light from surrounding waters,
blackening them as if to isolate
its own strangeness and underline
its silence. As with sheer coastal walls
that break rollers to nothings of froth
and bubbles, such monsters loom on
the mind and stagger balance.

Wrapped in cloaks, hooded, frozen
in a silence of our own, we stood with
hands clamping the rails against such
malignant loveliness. Over the ruins
of portals, cliffs, towers and melting
bridges, glazed dunes—for this too
was ice—colors slipped and played.
Fragilest blues. From vast interior
halls, greens fiercer than any bush
or tree's. Sapphires. Crystals.
Violent emeralds on undersea ledges,
all reflecting upward onto walls
and ceilings. Streams broke from above
and fell in rills to the ocean.

— Let us pull around this island awhile,
I said, and see what we can of it.

With Conor at the bow for floating ice
or shelves that might slice the skin,
we rowed within a few boat-lengths of it.
It gave off cold as well as lights, its face
here blue as June, there greeny white,
with darker greens under the dripping
overhangs, and sea ripple glittering it

everywhere in grottoes, under bridges,
a music of light on a vast smashup of
towers and caves, galleries and walls.
Whale-nosed juts bearded with icicles
protruded through in places.

— We'll go in here, I ordered at a wide
breach in the ice, for I saw that we could
bring the boat about in a baylet there
if no way through appeared.

— Father! several gasped.

— Have we come so far to turn away from
this? I roared, and took an echo
off the walls that shook me. Then
quietly I reminded my sons how
our hearts had brushed the rough skin of
eternity while a white-browed whale
cruised the vessel, his nose full of the smells
of sheep grease and ourselves. That time
I was killed with terror the while myself
until the beast dropped off our track,
and tempted to cry out to Manannan
or the Daghda, anyone but the Mother of God.

Many's the time, quaking under my cloak
like a calf who knows he's appointed for meat,
I admonished my brothers for their fear
and accused their faith while my own
turned thin as mist on a wall
and my resolve melted like snow off ditches.
Worse, at times I was afraid I'd revealed
my doubts to that sea-keeping boat.

So let us not have it that all the night
my mother thrashed in her blood to give me
to this world, the woods behind our rath
flamed in sign of my selection and by
daylight not a leaf's edge was singed—
nothing like that if you believe your soul
hangs by the single thread of the truth.

That sea is the lid of hell, and wore
an old face on its first morning.
In your ugliest night on a stone floor
you can't dream what's down there: squid
so great our whole community couldn't
stuff one in our oratory; fish
all swollen head, tall as you and four times
your bulk; lumps with fins; mouths
you could drive a donkey through; wide,
flat, winged things with eyes on their backs
and tails like oxen. Things you'd think
crawled from the Cave of Cruachan, but
I'll tremble you with them no more.
Instead I'll tell you a psalm I made
after many a sea with the ghost
of a mountain in every wave:

Doctor of our hearts, now we are as
murderers cast adrift, and would
gladly change vessels with sailors
on some glassy tide, who see
beneath them the boar-headed,
swallow-tailed ones turning bellies
pale as the drowned toward them,
and ones like swollen chestnut husks
and pincered, and other ribbony ones,

many-legged, tusked, lugworms
a weakening mind magnifies. For now
you raise a black wind from the north,
or send against us a gray west wind,
and we long for the barking of a fox
from a field's threshold after
first nocturn. Openmouthed on the edge
of every wave, we are lifted toward heaven.
Then—as our bellies drink our souls
like liquid fire—dropped
to a narrow glen. The light is
in turmoil, and our wits are useless
as cups of thrown water. We stagger this
way and that, take hold like men
by drink taken hold of and cry out
in our trouble, and hope down into the oak,
which groans for its roots again.
Each stringer of ash, bound ankle and wrist
in thongs, is a captive without reprieve,
crying out for the north side of
the mountain and a thrush at its berries.
The tree our saws drew the least
scantling from was seeded by Your hand,
and the oak's heart in our rails.
Even the ox hides we tanned in pits
of oak bark and stitched
with threads of flax, and wool grease
we slathered on our sheep-smelling hull
to keep the sea out. Therefore
our boat is from Your hand, *is*
Your right hand under us when we forsake
every heart-softening face—our white
martyrdom—for the emptiness of this
seal pasture where every angel-haunted
abbey stone sinks out of memory
and the salt blears consolations of
heather and harebell, things grown
large in our eyes. Clench Your fingers

in each stitch of flax as You did
in the roots when the weed flowered
blue against darker, wind-worked loughs,
for our mast whips sky, and our sail
is a fleeing rag. As You put breath
in the ox, breathe now with our
sea-trampler flexing its ribs to fit
water, Your eyes quick for the first
drips from faults the warblefly made
when this beast-boat plowed our fishless
fields, for we sail from bowl to bowl,
dragging the world with us, uphill
in all directions while our souls
touch bottom, longing for meadow-quiet
and a sea reflecting stars, not this
wave-beheading wind wherein the steersman
dares not look astern, but hangs like
a bug on a straw, and petrels creep
up the sides of the water.

We rowed into that cavern, then on
to a second. But for icicles plipping
and clear rills pattering down
it was quiet, the surface mild.
We moved through a honeycomb of ice,
chamber opening to chamber, each with its
own arrangement of those greens and blues.
Above, a sky swept of clouds. At every turn
I expected we'd be thwarted, ice arches
and walls closing so we'd have to take her
stern first out the way we came
and bring her about in a roomier vault.
But cavern after cavern appeared for us.

— Look. At the bow Conor pointed to a span
we were about to pass beneath.

What a thud to my heart! Two yellow eyes
up there watched us, unblinking,
bright as lamps in the ice.

— What do you make of it? I said, once
I had returned to myself.

— Now you have brought us to the silver castle
behind the north wind, where souls
are conducted after death, screamed Owen at me.

I hadn't recalled dying, I was about
to tell him, or ask if he'd drunk salt water
or seen the Black Pig, anything to draw
that poison from his mind with laughter,
and settle the crew, when something
up there took wing and carried those eyes off
with it, no doubt from Owen's noise,
and slipped across to settle on a further
ledge, leaning a little as it studied us.

— A bird, I said. Some big owl, I'd guess.

— But it's white! protested Owen.

— Well, it's white and it looks like
an owl, so I'd say it's an owl. *Big* white owl.
Why not call it down with one of your
fine songs?

Cernan and the others shook at this, with
laughter and relief, and the bird

pumped off soundlessly to another height,
turning its demeanor on us again,
more flustered than anyone but Owen,
whose face hung red between fury
and abashment like some boy's.

We were closer to land than I thought,
since there wasn't a lesser bird or mouse
an owl could live on there, but to take
the slack from a long rope, that bird
stayed with us as though on a tether
until we picked our way to open sea
on the farther side. Soon a wind for the south
banged into our sail. I missed that
caverned waste and its yellow-eyed spirit
when coastlines poked through the gray monotonies
we engaged later, and then concealed their forms.

God mend your head if you believe
I can reckon those distances or render them up
in days. As the flying bird can't hatch her eggs,
so bailing from one day through another,
chipping ice one-handed off the bow
while spray dashes it back on—
keeping her off bold shores the while—
crosses a spear with a sword
in a man's bones, cracks or flattens
his hours till day and night are one,
which in that North they are: at midnight
I have picked lice off my shirt up there
as handily as at noon. What a man
on the water wants is stars after sunset,
and to see ahead what's there
before dealing with it closely, not
a single evergreen leaning east from

a surf-bashed tumble of rocks, then gone
in mist, and again a red-faced cliff
closed over and shifted about and dragged out
further along. And don't be putting it down
in your thorny script that I foresaw
what was coming before we ever crossed horizon
to it. Any old hand knows mare's tails
on a blue-greeny pale sky mean big winds
in the offing. Same for a sunset the color
of whin blossoms, or a ring around the moon.
Ugly bottom creatures coming up for air
mean ugly weather, too, and an oily sea
that sets my joints to stabbing.

What islands we found, we found. Nameless,
unpeopled, without magical springs
except the luck of sweet bubbling water
sometimes, among cress and good roots
that let us graze awhile when we were ready
to drop, our strength poured out in our bailers,
and hollow from hours at the oars. May I not
give you scandal in saying that what fasts
we could we kept, but the day of the week's
the first land gear jettisoned out there.
Slack water bags enforced our fast days,
and provisions with seas washing in their sacks.

When we could we feasted, knowing thinner
days could be at hand when they would,
our cauldron going above Cernan's charcoal pan,
the fishheads given first to him as smith.
There were island grapes like undersized
pebbles at times, enough for a tight belly,
but keep miracles out of it. Don't edify those
grapes to the girth of apples. Day by day

the mist warmed so our cloaks were left aside
more and more, and stone-block islands
passed us by, risky for running a curragh up to.

As to the matter of this finny delusion
which I see you've given a name—
this Jasconius. This sleeping whale
you've written I let my brothers
tie the boat up to, build fires upon,
and celebrate mass on its back, returning
to it every Easter—I won't allow us
dressed up in nonsense that denies
simple sense as well as truth.

What might sound good in Rome makes me out
the witless navigator. A whale's back
is spotted, scarred-over where it isn't
barnacled, and looks nothing like
any land or stone I've set foot on, nor
is its flesh consistent enough to be mistaken so.
You're too long under this roof and need
constant airing if you think you're improving
anything with such elaborations.

Would I risk our hope of keeping from the waves
that way? No dead whale, either. Even then
it would be a stinking landfall no sailor
would get near, let alone anchor on.
What with sharks ripping gobbets off its pelt
so he'd barely get his soul back over the rail
with him, and seabirds picking it over
for a year or so, feasting it down to bones,
there'd barely be room for a wren

to step around on it. Though I'm in a tight
clutch with the years, I go back on
the clear-skied track of my thoughts,
so no more miracles, no dreaming whales
and no gryphons, either.

Brother Donal may cross strains
of cattle, but nobody's crossed a lion
with an eagle but you—and I want the gryphon
gone, not the excuse you're scribbling figurative,
for it was no gryphon carried poor Diarmuid
out of it, but the paw of a rogue wave,
since one moment he was there by the bow,
and the next, not. Only that salt tedium
circling and circling, and Diarmuid gone
for his mouthful of sand. Wasn't I in
a hundred pieces over it, as always?
Aren't I now? That put an end to restlessness
and sets me daily on my knees
in the river, saying my hours and fishing
for Diarmuid's soul with my prayers

So make me no miracles. I am no saint but
a gambler with souls not my own, despite my mouth
being full of high gab about the edge of
danger in all doings worth their time,
and standing in the gap. The night arrives,
long as the day has been. Owen, you'd guess,
was first to have the blame in his nose for me.
And you'd be wrong: as if his sickness was
going around, it was young Conor and Martin—
at the oars, greasing the hull when we'd haul up
on a strand. I'd just make out some
twist of a phrase—nothing long enough
to tie a cat with—about that yellow-eyed

owl or facing out of the creek cursed by
magpies or blue goats, all that old choke
sailormen fall back on when something like
Diarmuid's death can't be explained.

You can't put an old head on young shoulders,
well I knew, and would wait them out
unless things got so we were down
at the end of sense and into each other's faces.
Best in a sea-drift curragh to think of
all that brine and overlook what you can,
walk away from it in your mind, lest it infect
and you end trying the blasphemy of walking
away from it on water like some moorhen. That'd be
your miracle if you could pull it off.

Only think of each man memorizing the same
five faces over and over, week on,
week off, wrinkle and wart and black tooth
until beards and hair thicken and spread
and blessedly obscure them. The same five
voices as month piles up on month and years
collapse with the weight of them. There's
no escape on curraghs, not even to ease
your bowels. Not even in sleep, where
you'll hear, "Diarmuid, would you get your
blessèd elbow out of my blessèd mouth!"

And believe me or don't, it's worse when
there's no dirty weather to keep heads off
fleabites and the screaming bilge reek.
When the wind's fair, it's never fair enough

but they'll be thinking with their bellies
on fresh mutton joints and feast-day cups,
and the taller worries build, the softer
the abbot speaks, and doesn't dare turn
a sharpened word against one or another's
sea skills. You know when a brother
breaks wind and nobody yells, "Beware aft!"
that your crew's in trouble.

But did I never tell you of our run
to Inishdhugan for the clay, and of
Dhugan himself, that hard, unbelieving man?
Not long from this land here the boat's
full complement of fleas discovered us,
despite our regular dippings of the flesh
in salty coves and river mouths.
Some they enjoyed more than others,
and those had from them constant generous
rings around their wrists, ankles,
necks even, thick as king's-gift torques.

—What sort is this Dhugan? I'd asked Owen,
who suggested that since we'd be passing
anyway, we put in at his island
for this clay he had. A handful sprinkled
round would drive all vermin over the rails
to the sea like Gadarene swine, he promised.

—A wee, scarce man, Dhugan is, he said,
and one to be cagey with, for he'll take
no gift for his clay, though it has the power.

And sure enough, when we made landfall,
off on the end of a promontory

we found his walled place. A couple of
old wives skulked around among his stones
and sheep, and the great man himself
sat out to the sun before his hut,
cracking a pile of limpets, a withered fellow
grown but to my shoulder, of questionable age,
whether venerable or whitened early
from a profligate life I couldn't say.

— Remember, Owen whispered, he can't be accosted
in a trifling manner. Let me try.

— In the name of Balor the One-eyed, give me
some clay! he called out, stepping forward.

Did I tell you this was that same island
where Balor dwelt in those old stories?
Anyway, this Dhugan picked a limpet
off the heap and eyed it all over.

— What clay would that be? he asked, never
looking up even to count the extent of us.

— Your Honor's wonderful earth that a mere
fistful sends the rats hurrying from
the grain's vicinity, and clears boatloads
of lice off the premises.

— No clay I know of has the qualities
of that, Dhugan replied. It was barely
a mutter, delivered sideways.

— Sir, I said, thrusting my face into it,
I am Brendan, Abbot of Clonfert, and
these are five of my brethren.

We are sailing the seas for an island
proper for monks to contemplate God upon,
away from the traps and giddy toys
that pilfer the earthly time of men.
We beg a little of your clay to cleanse
our curragh of lice and fleas,
and offer in its stead our prayers
for your soul and its approaching journey.

— That is a thought too deep for me to wade in,
he said. But answer me this, if you can:
Why, if you're serving this God of yours,
for so you say, doesn't He send these bugs off
with a mere wave of His hand?

— It is not our business to question His ways,
I answered, and not a little too smoothly,
I might admit to you here, so I feared
I'd botched our chances for the clay, then turned
on myself at the thought I was allowing
this runt of the human litter to have his
play with me. I'd sooner be good grazing for
the vermin than cross more words with him,
I was about to tell him, when he spoke up again.

— Well, riddle me this then. I move
what cannot move itself. Though none can
see me, all bow down to me. What am I?

— God! one of the brothers whispered behind me.

— Yes, God! the others encouraged.

— Almighty God, I answered smiling at
the thought I'd cornered him now.

— The wind, he answered with a smirk.

— It could as well be true of the one
as the other, Cernan spoke up.

— Not if there is no other, said this
pointy-eared pagan dwarf, and at that
I took another step forward.

— You are singularly starved for imagination
if you truly believe what your mouth
just uttered, I said. Cernan laid a firm
hand on my arm to stay my anger.

— Well, answer me this then. I'm gray
some places, and blue, and red, and other
places green. When I die I do not die,
but make many more faces that were met
in me when I was one, who now am many.

— The sea, Cernan whispered in my ear.

— Try the soul! It must be the soul,
I heard Diarmuid behind me.

— A great host in battle. This from Martin.

— This time you have built false leads into it,
I told Dhugan straight to his pebbly eyes.
There's no such thing on all the earth. Now
it's "yes" or "no" to a bit of your clay,
and we'll be off.

He bent and picked a stone from a pile at hand.
I was ready to topple on him when
he smashed it down hard on another
so it broke to pieces of all manner of colors,
even those he'd put into his riddle.

— The answer is, this stone. Who lacks
imagination now? And might a solid man
like yourself be capable of the Salmon Leap?

My crew was sniggering at my back, not
all of it directed at this convoluted fellow.
I shrugged by way of saying I was
through with him, which he interpreted as
asking for a demonstration.

— It goes like this, he said, and laid his
ropy body flat down on his back, arms at his sides.

— The Salmon Leap! he announced, then curved
himself upward in a flash, so he was on his feet.

— Without bending your knees, he explained,
then dropped back down and showed us again.

One by one my brothers stepped forward
and performed the movement, each with
a measure of success I won't go into here,
all but Owen and myself. He wants to use us
awhile for his own beguilement, I'd decided.
Stuck on this island and not a praying man,
his sports were harmless, surely.

He ducked into his hut and came out quick.
Now we'll get the clay, I thought.

— One last trial, for certain, he said.
Stand this egg on its end and I'll
give over the clay.

It was coming on afternoon and I wanted
water under us before night was above us,
so stepped quick up and took the egg
in my palm, then went to a flat stone
on the wall and took the egg between thumb
and finger and set it fat end downward.
Need I say it rolled in a circle
until I trapped it again, and that each
brother repeated the situation? Get ready,
I cautioned myself, for next Dhugan'll
be breaking one end and sitting it in itself.

— Sure nobody who's come here yet can do
that one, Dhugan admitted, nor did he try himself.

— But wait and I'll get you the clay, he said.
No one's to follow.

Over the hill behind his hut at a trot
he went, looking back every three steps or so
to see we weren't on his track.
There's an island of speckled cursing stones
out there, so many no one ever counted
them twice but he got the different total.
Round and egg-shaped they are, and some
with carvings. You turn them left to right
for a good journey, and right to left,
against the path of the sun, to curse somebody.
They say if your curse is unjust it returns
on you like a stick with a bounce in it
tossed at a wall. Could we have found
that island I'd have risked it and turned
every pebble against that stringy little heathen
I'd prostrated my dignity to. The man was

mean as a stoat and three or four times
as cute, and not a louse or flea
swam for its life after we'd spread his dirt
about our hull. Nor would it surprise me
if that stuff wasn't the cause that
they seemed to double their coupling so more
climbed about on us than there are sheep
on summer mountainsides. It was no cure either
against those stinging bugs that flew at us
in the North, big as frogs and thick as
chaff the flail raises. Crawled over
and chewed on, it all'd make you wonder
just who the world was made for exactly.

Now as to your island of smiths,
let's bring it back down to earth and say
we passed a burning mountain or two
up there in the North, smoking away like
the turf was blazing good inside, then
roaring and sending up splashes of it so tall
its flaming sods sizzled the ocean about us
until we cleared away. We heard no anvils,
and no hairy men ran out and tossed fires
at us with tongs. These are what drink concocts
in the heads of old mariners whenever
landfolk can be seized by the earlobes
and held to hear them out, and are thus
unworthy of a monk's quill. Boat life taxes
men with long silences, and no crew loves
a windy comrade, therefore the natural
leaning toward ornament on shore. I've heard
such stories increase tenfold in color
and wonders with each retelling,
so what starts out a sprat
betimes gets inflated whaleward.

But there *is* a kind of fever that
can overtake a man after rolling long
on untenanted waters. It's not that he feels
strangely, but what he sees, which seems
always to be what he needs most. Without
warning and before he can be stopped,
a young brother's been known to get up,
walk forward to the bow and over, declaring
a woman there has given him the bashful look.

In my own case the fever began with
a jacksnipe baaing like a goat, impossible
out there. Then in clean daylight I saw
this very cashel wall, stone for stone on the sea,
and behind it our oratory with its west door
and its window slot set eastward, all these
clochans, the graveyard and monks' garden,
so real I might have plucked a cabbage leaf
to chew on. Brother Donal at his plow
raised a clutter of worm-hunting gulls
along the furrow at his back. I knew
his face. Meanwhile hawthorn whitened
all the world, heather wrestled with swine smell
and clover and the bread oven. I heard
wind clashing branches together where those oaks
lean away from the coast, and blackbirds.

Cernan and Owen caught me and held me down,
and in my tears I knew it wasn't the island
out ahead I wanted, but stone-ringed
Clonfert here behind us. The monk in harness
to his Lord, facing down the furrow of his duty.
Not this endless salt-plowing after every
wink of light at its edge. So when we shook
the fogs off and found that island,

I didn't go ashore, and forbade the others.
Tempted, as you'll see, but afraid the place
might keep me, that I'd never again hear our
sweet bell calling me to prayer a windy night.

Make note that I was the only one
who saw and heard what I saw and heard,
and can somewhat understand that the others
might doubt my word, given that they'd
had to take hold of things until I put myself
back together, though hadn't I led them
to that place without harm—Diarmuid excepting,
of course, whose poor fortune casts no mud
on anyone's over-assurance or neglect.
It was Martin and Conor, here at home,
scattered the tale I'd lost my sand
at the last of it and wouldn't go ashore
out of fear, so hatched the events
I'm about to lay out for you.

You know the way a bog-stained stream mingles
with a clear one? Between matins and prime
the night's like that—diluted with morning
so another twilight tricks the eyes.
Then it's better to trust your ears alone.
The boat laid-to, the sea quiet,
what I heard was a rush of air like
a shearwater whizzing past, then
a rustle like wings folding.

Visible or not, something was there
in the cockpit a few feet away,

in the stillness deepened by the sighing boat
and my crew snuffling and snoring
under sheepskins. Think of it. I might have
reached across and touched it—or him.
I didn't, though calm in my heart.

— Brendan.

— You know me then?

— Though you crossed by the skill of twelve
hands alone, I hung nine masts above you
all the way from the other side.

Oh that's a comfort, thought I, now that
it's over. Then hoped he hadn't power
to listen inside as well as out.

— Yesterday, he went on, when this landfall
seemed only a low blue cloud stretched
across the horizon, sighted on the moment
of each crest, lost with each drop to a trough,
before it rooted itself in the sea and every
weed patch and tern homing to it made it true,
before it separated to leafy woods above white dunes . . .

Tell me what I already know, I was
thinking, when he took a new tack.

— A long, starless night will drop
down the northern way that brought you here,
island to island as the traveler uses
stepping-stones to cross a stream. Men of
the bays, flying the hawk's banner:
red for the blood of your brothers-to-be,

staining pasture and strand; black for
the burnt stones of abbeys. The anchorite's bell
will ring out fainter and fainter on oceanic
silence, while thick-handed strangers fondle
the staff of Patrick and fair women,
and brute gods enthrone your altars. Then,
iron-chested ones sailing out of sunrise
to envenom the cup of peace. Sly as the goldwork
on a warrior's brooch, the little kings
will entangle son with father, brother against
brother. Where towers like dragon's teeth
remind the land a thousand years, bishops
will hunt the red deer instead of souls.
Then Christian bones, starved and staring,
walking the bogs and mountains, stripped of
everything from lambkin to mother tongue, even
the dirt that might clothe their rest.

I thought to waken Brother Owen to see if
he could unravel this jabber for me,
but feared this one's presence might set
the teeth of death in the old man.

— You seem bottomlessly endowed
with dire riddles, I told him. But say it
plain, since I'm long on years and won't
play what children's games I won't.

— When these things come to pass, your people
will need the sanctuary of places like this.
I say "your people" though none on your island
thinks himself part of a race, but only
a member of some narrow kingdom at war with
every other, and therein is the cause of this
coming nightfall—petty alliances with strangers,
the daughter sold in marriage for personal gain,
revenge of piddling, half-imagined slights.

— That is a sad truth. But tell me,
what place is this?

— Call it the land beyond the wave.
You are the first I've led here, but others
will sail across centuries to it.

— I praise God for it.

— Well you might, considering that lifelong
you have turned a cold face to the creation
He set you in to love and find Him through.
This world was complete without you, man,
or any of your kind. There is no reason
for you or anyone, and nobody's worthy
of this world, yet all whimper against it
as you do, wanting blue eyes if theirs
are brown, or a smaller nose or waist.
Half your race is walking around with
stiff nostrils as though each step sunk them
deeper in manure, while others figure—
oh the constant figuring! Here's one
over here figuring how to barter a field
for more bullocks to swap for a larger field
while that one over there's calculating
how to market his daughter to the son
of the other with all the bullocks
without throwing an extra field into
the bargain. Meantime this third fellow
with no bullocks or fields is looking
for ways to get the other two spitting
in their palms and shaking on the arrangement
so he can secure a field from the one
and a few bullocks for it from the other.
Go down to the strand and you'll find
another waving a stick above a heap
of shells, as if they'll turn gold
and shiny stones if he can only get

the motion right—and this the one time
they'll walk the world!
Never do they account that purely from
their Creator's largess they're here, not
from any excellence of their own.

He was in a fine ruffle. Best not to cross
talking points with this one.

— And your own little pile of shells is
that you've had both eyes on eternity
so long you've never thought to thank Him
for the marvels of your own creaturehood.
Smell it, man! Take a deep breath
for once in your life without fearing
you'll spring a rib through a lung
just for falling in love with the world.

Like a swung thurible or cauldron stirred,
breath of the simmering land
passed over the ship. Warmth the sand stored
in every grain, released on the night breeze,
tangible as a sail bellied all day
to the sun. Cedar. Pine resins drawn out
by the heat. A hint of clay under salt-blown
roses, then dankness rising from fallen leaves.
Nothing like mild Clonfert, but
such excess in my nostrils as almost
to knock me on my stern-end.

— Here where no man behind a wall
has dropped his ear in on his neighbor's
business yet, for a time the creation
will please its Maker with original

birdsong again. He drifts in wild-flower
pollen across your bow and strikes
tendrils from seeds and rain from clouds.
He is there in this startling vine fragrance
and in mud flats edged with rotting fish,
in fish rot and stone damp and rockweed
baking on sand. He's the purple,
blue, and maroon of berries you'll taste
behind that shore.

— I'll taste no berries over there,
nor dip a foot in those shallows. From here
we swing this boat sunward for home.

My boldness startled me as much as him, I think.
But now the stones were tumbled
and the horse was out the breach:

— My own pile of shells, is it? Larking around
in the sky while we're down here keeping
this curragh from drinking up the ocean,
sleeping so long under wet sheepswool we've turned
reeking leather satchels bagging our own guts?
Eating in the dark so we won't see
what's already eating what we're supposed to eat?
Wondering the while when our joints will swell
and lock so fleas and lice can pick us
to the marrow without fear of being scratched?
How many call *you* Father? I never took vows
to be abbot, but I got three thousand sons
anyway, in this world and the next, and right now
the full wet weight of a drowned one sitting
here on my heart. All because I set the second stone
on the first at Ardfert, Clonfert, Inchiquin,
and twenty other places, and spent my life
talking monks into staying around each year

when the oats were ready to come in, instead of
letting them traipse off home to comfort their
poor old mothers. *You* try playing Solomon
when one brother says a Connaught man
can resurrect a ram long enough
to get the trade done, and the other says
the scrawniest cat in Connaught would walk away
from a Munster trout, and it goes to "I piss
in your ear" and back and forth to unnatural
things about the other man's sister
and from there to knife points.

Thick as my neck was in those days, this angel—
if so he was, for *now* I remembered
the Evil One on the heights with Our Lord—
this winged creature closed hands around my neck
the way a gannet wraps both feet about
its unhatched egg, and shook me off the deck.

— Say it, man! Out with it!

And I, weak as a hen who sees her future
in the pot, but thinking of this Clonfert
my delirium had spread before me on the sea,
and getting out of that one's clutches
back here to it:

        O Lord
        I have loved
        the Glory of
        Your house

Notes

Page 2.   Although Clonfert Abbey was located in East Galway, the monks depart from what is now Brandon Creek, on the Dingle Peninsula, Kerry.

Page 11.   The Arctic Mirage, or Hillingar effect, as it is called in Iceland, is created when a quantity of cloudless, motionless atmosphere stabilizes over a much cooler surface and alters the optical character of the air so that it curves the light like an enormous lens. Landmasses far beyond the horizon then appear to be within sight, floating above the horizon, sometimes upside down or one above the other.

Page 32.   The fever Brendan experiences is usually called a calenture in sailing lore.

Glossary

BALOR. Balor of the Evil Eye, who was believed to have lived on what is now called Tory Island, the Inishdhugan where the monks sail for the clay. Balor's eye was so large and powerful it required four men to raise the lid. It could destroy an army with one look.

BELTANE. May Day, the beginning of Irish summer, which is celebrated with bonfires.

CASHEL. The stone wall surrounding the monastic property, meant in a legal sense to define the sanctuary and to serve as a barrier against intrusion.

CAVE OF CRUACHAN. The entrance to the Other World.

CLOCHAN. A circular stone "beehive" hut.

DAGHDA. Literally, "Good God," a pagan deity of wisdom, whose cauldron was endlessly bountiful and one end of whose club was used to kill the living, the other to bring the dead back to life.

MANNANAN. "Son of the Sea," the chief pagan Irish sea-god.

ORATORY. An oblong stone chapel, in shape like an overturned boat.

RATH. A circular earthwork mound inside a ditch or moat, within which an extended family lived. In stony areas, a wall with no ditch was substituted. Also called a ringfort, either sort was as much a containment for livestock as a defense against attack.

SHEEP ISLANDS. The Faroes.